A Fish Named Dowg

Author: Fannie Lewis Barnes
Illustrator/Publisher: Gaurav Bhatnagar

This book is the property of:

To: ______________________

From: ____________________

Date: ____________________

Message:

ISBN – 9781737657170

Printed – The United States of America

This book is dedicated to my cousin, Eric. He inspired me to write about his Tropical/ Oscar fish due to some of the "out of the ordinary" behaviors that he observed from the fish.

As I listened to Eric's narratives concerning some of the actions of his pets, I could hear the excitement in his voice as he talked and laughed about the way one fish in particular acquired its name.

I feel it only befitting to dedicate this book to my Comical Cousin, Entertaining Eric.

I would like to thank my family, individually as well as collectively for their continued support and encouragement.
God Bless!!!! (Author)

This narrative also includes:

Overall Objective
Words to Know
Definitions and Information
Silly, Strange Story
Reading with Rhyming
Points to Ponder
Fun-filled Facts
Teachable Tools
Lessons to Learn
Workable Worksheets
Skilful Suggestions

Even though this story is designed to be funny and enjoyable, it is also designed to be informative.
Upon reading this story, we should give notice as to how and what people can learn from these fish.

Overall Objective

The overall objective of this narrative is to provide purposeful interesting information to assist in improving reading and comprehension skills to:

motivate the mind
reinforce reading
exhibit enjoyment
strengthen skills
promote purpose
challenge change
boost the brain

While allowing the thinking process to be put into practice with ERIC.

Enjoy
Read
Improve
Comprehend

Words to know

1. Dowg
2. Oscar
3. Albino
4. Spike
5. E'Rock
6. tropical
7. aquarium
8. rearrange
9. similarity
10. difference
11. environment
12. diverse
13. ordinary
14. lesson
15. unique

Definitions and Information

~ fish – a cold-blooded animal that lives in water and has scales, fins, and gills.

~ fish/fishes – any of a large group of vertebrate animals that live in water, breathe with gills, and usually have fins and scales.

~ gill – either of the pair of organs near a fish's mouth through which it breathes by extracting oxygen from water.

~ gill – an organ (as of a fish) for taking oxygen from water.

~ fin – a part on the body of a fish shaped like a flap that is used for moving and steering through the water.

~ fin – any of the thin parts that stick out from the body of a water animal and especially a fish and are used in moving or guiding the body through the water.

~ aquarium (uh-kwair-ee-uhm) - a glass tank in which you can keep fish.

* You can use the word "fish" or "fishes" when referring to different species of fish; however, the fish in this story are of one species (Oscar Fish).

Definitions and Information (cont)

~ aquarium – a container (as a tank or bowl) in which fish and other water animals and plants can live.

~ tropical fish (trah-pi-kuhl) - any of various small or brightly colored fish that originally come from the tropics.

~ tropical fish – a small usually brightly colored fish often kept in aquariums with warm water.

~ similarity (sim-uh-lar-i-tee) – the quality of being similar or alike; (the i has the short i sound).

~ similarity – the quality or sate of being alike in some way or ways.

~ difference (dif-ur-uhns or dif-ruhns) – a way in which one thing is not like another.

~ difference – what makes two or more persons or things not the same.

~ diverse (di-vurs or dye-vurs) – having many different types or kinds;

~ diverse - different from each other.

* Readers can observe the similarities and differences of the definitions from these books: (Merriam-Webster's Elementary Dictionary) and (Scholastic Children's Dictionary). **The Accented Syllables are from the Scholastic Children's Dictionary.

R	E	A	D
R	E	A	D
e	n	n	e
l	j	d	v
a	o		e
x	y		l
			o
			p

R E A D

Relax with this book
Enjoy it from the shelf,
And you will see that you can
Develop skills all by yourself!

Rate this unusual story as
Explained to you by me,
About pet tropical Oscar fish
Dowg the friendliest of the three.

A Fish Named Dowg

Little readers, what I am about to do
Is reveal a story that I have for you.
From the owner's and the fish's point of view,
Let it be known if you think it is true.

Readers, are you ready to begin?
You can read alone or with a friend,
With teacher, para, parent or kin
More rhyming will be penned near the end!

From: The Author

Are you ready to read this (fab-yuh-rif-ik) story? This means that you should find this story to be fabulous and terrific! Let us begin!

“Hello readers”

“I am Eric/Little Ric”

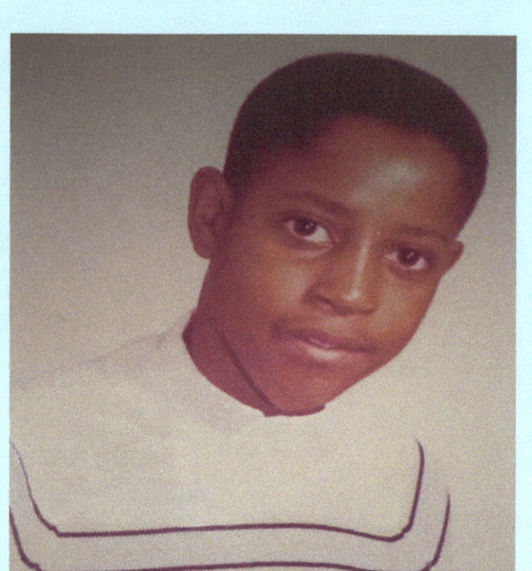

“I am E’Rock”

“I am Spike”

“I am Dowg”

Far, far away in a land called Cleveland, there live three pet fish. These fish live with their human owner, Eric. In this story Eric will be called, "Little Ric" from time to time. Eric's fish are Tropical fish also known as Oscar fish.

These fish occupy a large aquarium also called a fish tank. The tank contains: fish and water of course; filter, air pump, light, plants, thermometer, rocks, pebbles, rock house, a wooden barrel and other nice decorations.

Once Eric received these fabulous fish he was determined to give his pet fish their appropriate names. He looked at them and paid close attention to their behaviors. As you read, you will find out why and how each fish acquired its name.

We are Spike, Dowg and E'Rock
Without any doubt,

We are the friendly Oscar fish
You will be reading about.

First, the brave black fish is named Spike because of the spike like points on its body. Secondly, the pleasant pink Albino fish is named E'Rock because it is strong, yet friendly. Then there is the other fish; its name is, well, I will tell you exactly how this fish acquired its name.

You will meet these fish shortly, just keep reading and you will soon find out about the unique one.

On one fabulous sunny day, Eric knew that it was time to feed his fish, so he walked over to the aquarium with the fish food in his hand. Just as he was about to put the food into the tank, one of the fish jumped up to the top of the water as if trying to get the food out of Eric's hand. As soon as the fish did this, Eric said, "He almost bit my hand!" "He tried to bite me like a dog!" "That's it! I have the perfect name for this fish; I will name this one Dowg!" He knew that the name had to be spelled differently from that of a real barking dog, so he pondered and wondered; then he decided to spell the fish's name, D-O-W-G! Now, readers, you know why and how this particular fish acquired its name.

Initially, it was believed that Eric was talking about a real dog because he said that his pet jumped up and tried to bite him and that the pet seemed to do other tricky things as well.

This particular fish, Dowg did more, was more outgoing and was more active than the other two fish, Spike and E'Rock. Dowg rearranged some of the items in the aquarium because the fish did not like the way Eric had it decorated.

During another fine fabulous sunny days, Dowg took the plants and moved them behind the rock house. The next day the plants were moved to the left side of the rock house. The day after that, Dowg moved the plants to the right side.

As Eric was checking on his fish, not only did he see Dowg moving things around, but he saw that Dowg had collapsed, knocked down the rock house and had hidden some food behind the plants and the house.

Day after day and night after night Dowg would move, rearrange and change things around in their aquarium. Soon Eric realized that Dowg and perhaps the other fish did not enjoy having all of the items in their tank; so guess what? Eric removed the rock house and some of the plants from the aquarium. Do you think this made Dowg and the other fish sad? No! They were not sad, they were happy because they did not want all of the decorations in their aquarium.

Dowg did a good thing by not giving up until the change was good and it made their environment better. Now that some of the plants and other items have been removed from the tank, Dowg, Spike and E'Rock have enough room to swim faster, play, eat and have more fun!

Since these tropical fish are smart, they know when it is time to be fed. Whenever they see Eric coming toward them with their food, they will jump up and do their "happy feeding dance." This is when they will get to the top of the water and will swim back and forth really, really fast. Of course, Dowg will jump higher and swim faster than the other fish.

On one terrific sunny day, Little Ric was asked to take pictures of Spike, E'Rock and Dowg. As he was doing so, he noticed that Dowg looked at the camera, then looked at the other fish as if to say, "Come on friends, let's get in this picture before I swim away!" Once the pictures were taken, Little Ric noticed that Dowg looked at the other fish again, but this time it seemed as if Dowg said, "Although you were in the picture, this story is mostly about me; however, I do not mind sharing the spot light with you because we all are fabulous fishy friends."

On the same terrific sunny day, Eric paid close attention to how well Dowg, Spike and E'Rock played together and how they ate and swam together, seemingly with little to know problems.

During the time that Little Ric was observing his fish, he noticed some of the diverse things about them; some differences such as their shapes, sizes, behaviors, their different attitudes and their different colors. Then, all of a sudden, Little Ric noticed something more important than the differences in these fish, he noticed their many similarities; things that these fish have in common or ways in which they are alike. He noticed things such as their gills, fins, scales, their eyes, their swishy tails, he noticed how smart they are, he also noticed how the good

deed from Dowg seemed to be appreciated once the rearranging in the aquarium was done.

Readers, do you know what? Little Ric noticed more similarities than differences. In spite of the differences in Spike, Dowg and E'Rock, it is believed that these fish realize some of the things they have in common; they are tropical fish, known as Oscars, but they are identified individually, yet classified as fish.

Eric thought about how these different or diverse ways did not separate or stop E'Rock, Spike and Dowg from swimming around, eating, playing and having fun together. Suddenly, Little Ric started to ponder and wonder; then a question came to his mind. The question was, "If these fish, with their similarities, yet their differences can inhabit, yes, live in the same place and get along with each other, why can't people with their differences and similarities learn to live together and get along with each other?"

Learners, you will probably be surprised at the good things you can do once you put your mind to it.

It was surprising yet hard to believe some of the things that Dowg did as well as some of the things that Oscar fish can do. The curiosity in learning more about the different actions and behaviors of these type fish became very interesting. Therefore, these fun facts were found for you. Did you know?

Fun-Facts about Oscar fish:

- **There are several types of Oscar Fish, some of which are: Tiger Oscar, Albino Oscar, Golden Oscar or Lemon Oscar Fish.**
- **They can recognize their owner by their hand (this is one of the signs of their smartness or intelligence).**
- **They can redesign or redecorate their tank according to their liking by moving things around.**
- **They have two sets of teeth; one set is in the back of their mouth and the second set is located in their throat.**
- **They can jump up or out of the tank (usually when they see something to eat above the tank).**
- **They have a unique personality (sometimes they will play dead). They can be taught to do tricks.**
- **Because of their behavior they are also named as river dogs or water dogs).**

What interesting, fun-filled facts about Oscar fish!

You've finished that part of the story
Please read it one more time,
Of Spike, Dowg and E'Rock
This time you'll read the rhyme!

Now notice the similarities
And differences between the two,
Then as you ponder and wonder
Decide which is preferred by you.

As you read the same narrative
Compare them from beginning to end,
Then decide which version is better
For you to comprehend.

This is not your ordinary story
Of ordinary fish, I must say,
The setting is in a different town
In a place far, far away.

This story is of three Oscar fish
Somewhat different, somewhat the same,
You'll learn about the active one
And how it acquired its name.

Eric, the owner was feeding his fish
And he counted one, two, three,
Then he said, "One fish jumped up
I believe it tried to bite me!"

To the top of the aquarium
The fish jumped like a frog,
Eric said, "Although it is not
I will name this one, Dowg!"

The name spelling is different
From that of a real dog you see,
Notice the spelling, it's not dog
It is spelled D-o-w-g!

Friendly readers let's agree
The owner we will not blame,
For giving this unique Oscar fish
This strange unusual name.

These fabulous fish are tropical
They are very much alike,
The friendly fishy Oscar friends
Are E'Rock, Dowg and Spike.

Little Ric's favorite pets
Live in water not on dry land,
They know that it is time to eat
Whenever they see his hand.

They also know it's feeding time
When they see him at a glance,
As soon as he gets close to them
They will do their happy dance!

Little Ric cares about his fish
And they do care about him,
He treats all of his fish the same
Yes, all three of them.

These fish swim and eat together
In their large comfortable tank,
But for the nice decorations
They have their owner to thank.

Their aquarium has a rock house
And the pebbles which are plenty,
Other items are in the tank
Readers, can you think of any?

Of course Dowg did move some things
During the day and during the night,
They were moved to the left side
Behind and to the right.

Dowg moved the rock house
And some of the food it hid,
The other fishy friends approved
Of exactly what Dowg did.

As Dowg rearranged specifics
Eric observed as he sat,
He saw the changes Dowg made
And the other fish were okay with that.

Eric removed some things entirely
But others, only disposed of some,
Now, the fish have room to swim
In their nice aquarium.

Little Ric then noticed the look
Of approval on the fish's face,
Their environment is much better
Since everything is in its place.

There are facts about these fish
As you heard from the start,
The Oscar fish are very unique
And they are very smart!

People and fish are somewhat different
Yet, they have similarities,
They have some things in common
A few things such as these.

They have mouths, eyes and lungs
And they all need to eat,
But people walk, fish do not
Fish do not have feet.

Learning to live together
Whether different or alike,
Is what people should try to do
As E'Rock, Dowg and Spike.

Little Ric pondered and wondered
Saying, "Readers, I have this wish,
That people will try to get along
With each other like these fish!"

If people desire to get along
They have to try it first,
Living in unity can be achieved
Even though people are diverse.

Change and rearrange things
Only when you should,
Do it to help others and
yourself Whenever it is for the good.

Words and definitions like people
Can be diverse also,
Once you focus on similarities
The more you'll learn and will know.

Did you notice some similarities
Of definitions in front of this book?
Now, notice some of the differences
As you take another look.

Despite diversities in people or fish
Doesn't matter how they look,
Hopefully you learned and enjoyed
Something from this unusual book!

Now that you've read everything
That the author had to tell,
Perhaps you'll want to become
A fine fabulous friend as well.

Dowg waited to talk to listerners
Here at the very end,
Of the story about this active fish
Along with E'Rock and Spike the friends.

Read what this Oscar fish might say
To the followers and to the leaders,
Here is this dialogue by Dowg
With more information for the readers.

After which enjoy the skill sheets
From what the author said,
About Eric, Dowg, Spike, and E'Rock
From this story you have read.

A Fish Named Dowg

"Hello, my name is Dowg
A pet dog and I aren't the same,
I am not the kind that barks
Observe the spelling of my name."

"I do not walk, I do not run
I do not eat from a dish,
I swim in the nice tank all day
Because I am Dowg, the fish!"

"My friends and I do get along
In our aquarium where we all fit,
Although it was decorated by Eric
I rearranged some things in it."

"Now, Spike, E'Rock and I
Are comfortable and content,
We learned to live together
In our own environment!"

"We get along, we do not argue
Of course we do not fuss,
We, the fabulous fishy friends
Hope you enjoyed reading about us!"

"You know about our fish fins
You know about our gills,
Let's see how much you know
About the following learning skills!"

Draw and Color pictures of the Fabulous Fishy Friends

Draw lines to match the same words.

1. similarities	tank
2. differences	aquarium
3. unique	rearrange
4. aquarium	differences
5. tank	acquired
6. diverse	tropical
7. rearrange	friends
8. friends	unique
9. tropical	similarities
10. acquired	diverse

Fill in the blanks with the correct missing letters.

f ___ s ___	fish
t a ___ k	tank
O___ c ___ ___	Oscar
A___ b i n ___	Albino
E’ ___ ___ c k	E’Rock
S p ___ k ___	Spike
D ___ w g	Dowg
p l ___ ___ t	plant
g i ___l	gill
s ___ i ___	swim

Write these words in ABC Order

1. Dowg	1. ______________
2. Oscar	2. ______________
3. Tropical	3. ______________
4. Spike	4. ______________
5. E'Rock	5. ______________
6. aquarium	6. ______________
7. similar	7. ______________
8. different	8. ______________
9. fin	9. ______________
10. gill	10. ______________

Circle the words in each row that are the same.

ponder	story	book	ponder
unique	active	unique	fish
terrific	look	Spike	terrific
wonder	wonder	Oscar	many
common	read	common	facts
people	people	sunny	learn
enjoy	E'Rock	pets	enjoy
swim	Dowg	swim	room
change	change	different	alike
search	notice	skills	search

Skilful Suggestions

1. Ask reader to point to or give the author's and illustrator's initials or names.
2. Ask reader the title of this book.
3. Ask reader to name the three fish in this story.
4. Ask reader what is Little Ric's other name?
5. Have reader point to, repeat, or pronounce words from the "Words to Know" list with prompting or independently.
6. Have reader trace or re-write words from the "Words to Know" list and/or look up words.
7. Have reader to name or write similarities and/or differences in fish and people. Example: (people and fish have eyes; people walk/have feet; fish swim/do not have feet).
8. Ask reader to give some of the listed facts about Oscar Fish.
9. Ask what sources did the author use to search for definitions as well as information about Oscar fish? (website and books)
10. Have reader to complete skills according to his/her functioning abilities.

<u>I hope you readers, listeners and learners enjoyed this:</u>

~ aquarium action
~ tank tails
~ water wiggling
~ room rearranging
~ utterly unusual
~ silly story
~ featuring fabulous fishy friends

Readers, will you rate this story
From beginning to the end?
You will receive this Big 10 award
If you rate this story a 10!!

"BIG 10 AWARD"

(Reader's Name)
Presented the "BIG 10 AWARD"
For listening to the very end,
And being such a friendly reader
Thus rating this story a 10!
Learned about these Oscar fish
Of their scales, gills and fins,
Dowg, Spike and E'Rock
The smart helpful fishy friends!

Date

Adult Guide's Signature

Data

*Website:

aquagoodness.com
Oscar Fish Facts (Fun and Interesting) Tom Jones, 2020.

**Books:

Merriam-Webster's Elementary Dictionary.
Merriam-Webster, Incorporated. 2019.
Scholastic Children's Dictionary. Produced by Potomac Global Media, LLC. 2019.

***Remember: "There is a need; you need to read!"

Author's Information

Email: morepsplease@gmail.com
Facebook: Fannie Lewis Barnes
Amazon.com: Books by Fannie Lewis Barnes

Author's published books on Amazon are:

~ I Must Read - Curriculum/Common Core Standards Based Material, (Alphabets A-Z, pictures, long/short vowels, simple sentences, instructions)

~ Reading As I Learn R.A.I.L. – (Counting 1-10, number words, colors, color words, pictures)

~ Ray and Mae / Bringing Smiles – (Best Bunny Buddies making everyone and everything happy with their presence)

~ My Little Friends – (Different baby animals)

~ Let's Stick Together – (Friends sticking together)

~ Once Upon A Time- (A story about talking insects)

~ I Like Likeable Things – (Different foods, games, sports, etc. that different children like)

*Books include Skilful Suggestions and Worksheets

www.ingramcontent.com/pod-product-compliance
Lightning Source LLC
LaVergne TN
LVHW070151110826
845147LV00002B/372

* 9 7 8 1 7 3 7 6 5 7 1 7 0 *